FIELD BARNS OF
THE PEAK DISTRICT

By Long Rake, Youlgrave

Sheila Hine

Sheila Hine

Bottom Barn, Dale Farm, Grindon

ALL PHOTOS ARE BY THE AUTHOR UNLESS OTHERWISE CREDITED

CHURNET VALLEY BOOKS
1 King Street, Leek, Staffordshire. ST13 5NW 01538 399033
www.leekbooks.co.uk
© Sheila Hine and Churnet Valley Books 2013
ISBN 9781904546924
Printed by Delmar Press Colour Printers Ltd., Nantwich, Cheshire. Tel: 01270 624122

INTRODUCTION

Being a farmer with an interest in landscape photography, it's not surprising that field barns have attracted me. They sit in the landscape organically; usually made from locally sourced stone and often set in stunning scenery; a far cry from modern agricultural buildings of concrete and steel which although functional often sit as an uncomfortable scar in the landscape.

So I have become an 'anorak' of field barns and on finding a new one I wonder why was it built there - perhaps taking advantage of a slope, and where was the water - it might be a dew pond or mere in limestone country or a spring-fed trough, a brook or a stream in gritstone country.

Here in the Peak District we have a good variety of barns, from small limestone hovels, sheep shelters, even gritstone hencotes up to large estate barns. We might not be able to compete with the vast number of barns in the Yorkshire Dales but we still have a good number left although a lot have already gone completely from the landscape and many more are in various states of ruin.

Stone hencote, Quarnford

So this project is a capture of where we are now and a celebration of field barns before even more are lost back to nature or recycled into another building. Also to record the memories of some of the people who worked in them when they were used for the purpose they were built for, before they too are gone. I have a great respect for the farmers or their workers who slogged round these barns in winter, day in and day out in all weathers, especially to those barns in very exposed places.

I am indebted to all the people who have contributed information and to the farmers and landowners who have allowed me access to their land and barns, most of whom are very interested and fond of their barns; some being sad and frustrated that they are unable to afford to keep them in repair and some being angry that modern times are hastening the decline with the theft of roof slates and vandalism.

However with the aid of grant funding from schemes such as the Environmentally Sensitive Area (ESA) quite a lot of barns have been restored over the last 20 years so they should be safe for the next few decades. In the conclusion to this book I will question how we might proceed (or not) to keep a valuable landscape feature of the Peak District. In 1988 a report by SAVE Britain's Heritage commented that '*the Peak District without its traditional field barns would be a far less interesting landscape.*'

Most of the barns are on private property with no public right of access. However, for the visitor to the Peak District, a lot of the barns are visible from public roads and footpaths and this book should give an added interest and understanding of the landscape.

THE BACKGROUND

We share some of our barn heritage with the north, especially Yorkshire, well known for its many barns and for the Scandinavian influe[nce] which also came down into the Peak District. This is particularly noticeable around the Hope Valley where barns resemble the ones in North Yorkshire Dales with the prominent through stones and large barn doors, sometimes porched to allow a loaded cart to be pushe[d]

Cruck barn near Leek, demolished 1985

pulled under cover. This was perhaps more necessary in this wetter, more unsettled climate, than in the eastern or southern parts of the Peak District. In that area too, 'cote' is used more in the names, from the Viking tradition and I came across the use of 'baulks' for loft which is a common Yorkshire term. Another Scandinavian tradition was summering of stock in higher pastures where a cowman or shepherd might stay with the animals in a bothy. In Yorkshire the barns are often known as Laithes from the Old Norse 'hlatha' for barn. They are known as Fieldhouses in the northern Dales but around here it is barns, field barns or outer barns.

There would have been some cattle shelters going right back in time. Vaccaries or cattle farms are recorded as belonging to the wife of Edward 1, Queen Eleanor, who held Macclesfield until her death in 1290. In the 14th century a vaccary is recorded at Midgley near to Gradbach. This can also be picked up in the names of places like Hardingsbooth near Longnor, Birchenbooth, Quarnford and the Booths of Edale. Booth is from Old Norse for cattle farm where there would be housing for cattle and improved land for spring and autumn grazing and a hay crop to be taken du[ring] the summer while the cattle were away on summer pasture. An example would be the cattle of Alstonefield which used to go to the Ha[yes] in the southeast corner of Fawfieldhead, then known as Alstonefield Hayes which was common pasture for Alstonefield and Fawfieldh[ead]

Grimwith High Laithe, Yorkshire Dales.
400 year old cruck barn thatched with ling.

township. This was known as transhumance. The cattle were reared [to] provide oxen for ploughing and pulling carts, for dairy products, meat [and] hides.

There were also bercaries or sheep farms where sheep were kept [and] sometimes housed in long cotes to protect their fleece from bad weather. In [the] 14th century the wool trade was at its highest and half of the nation's we[alth] was founded on it. At this time various monasteries that had granges in [the] Peak District were producing high quality wool for export to Flanders and It[aly]

Early barns would be built using crucks of ash or sometimes oak. These w[ere] curved trees which could be used whole or split in half, joined at the top [with] a beam morticed between them to make a figure A. Two or more of thes[e] frames could be erected and joined together with a timber framework and [the] sides infilled with wattle and daub - interwoven branches smeared with mu[d or] clay and containing straw or animal hair to help bind it together. The r[oof] would be thatched with anything suitable to hand; reed, rushes or heathe[r]

farming developed further in the 1700s with crops such as turnips being grown to supplement the ration needed to sustain more animals over winter instead of killing so many in the autumn. More stock could be kept to breed in the next year so there could be a surplus of animals and produce to sell and provide a cash income instead of just subsistence farming. Demand grew too as towns developed and became more industrial. So it made sense to have a more substantial building to keep the animals in and be a better shelter for the fodder than just an outside stack in a harsh winter climate.

Ling Barn, Daggerstones, Healaugh, Swaledale.

A hogg house thought to be from the 17th century and restored in 2007 by Mr and Mrs J. Morrogh-Ryan

Ridgeway Barn on Hardenclough landholding, Edale. National Trust.

The common fields around villages were slowly being partially enclosed as field strips were being amalgamated, in some cases into larger allotments or closes, and walled, hedged or fenced off. The Parliamentary Enclosures from the 1750s to 1850s had a greater effect on changing the countryside and the majority of the field barns that we see today will have been built from that time especially in the 1800s.

It was a time of improvement where common and intake land was divided up and enclosed and people who had rights on the land could receive an allotment or parcel of land in lieu of their common rights. Some landowners had extra land added but poorer people might only have a small field allotted to them, if anything at all and possibly the poorer or less accessible land at that.

Many miles of walls were built and field barns of varying size and design constructed, depending on your status or ability. In some places, farms from the village would relocate to these new enclosures and a new farm-steading grow up.

The barns had developed into stone buildings; more substantial stone walls had been built which would support roof trusses which could then support the weight of stone slates. Now the roof had to be on a more shallow pitch, about 35 degrees to hold the slates whereas a thatched roof would have had a sharper pitch of about 60 degrees to shed rain water effectively. This would also increase the roof space for storage of fodder. It is sometimes possible to see evidence on a gable end of a building that the roof angle has been changed. The only barn that I have seen with a steep enough angle to have been thatched is near Magpie Mine, near Sheldon and now roofless (right).

The roof slates were usually held on with a hand-whittled oak peg though sometimes a piece of animal bone or a copper nail was used. Transport was needed to get stone which would split and layer out into suitable roof slates; large ones for the bottom rows could weigh up to one and a half hundredweight (75kilos). In the South West Peak 'grey slates' were cut at Flash, Goytsclough, Macclesfield Common, Pott Shrigley, Wincle, Reeve Edge, Danebower and Kerridge from where in 1416-17, 19 carts transported 2,000 'sclatestones' to Cheshire costing 6s 2d per thousand and an additional shilling for carriage.[1] At that time the slates would have been used on churches or substantial properties only.

From the 1850s onward with the development of rail transport, local materials could be added to with Welsh or Cumbrian slate, corrugated iron or Staffordshire Blue tiles, and more recently steel, asbestos and cement fibre. These materials made roofs cheaper and easier to repair than the heavy stone slates, and the carved stone ridges were, and are, hard to replace.

1. *The South West Peak: History of the Landscape.* Eric Wood (Ashbourne 2007)

Limestone is generally brittle and hard to work with, so in limestone areas barn walls are mostly of random construction but sandstone and gritstone being sedimentary is more easily worked and so more often coursed. Again this would depend on the funds available; whether good stone could be accessed or bought and stonemasons employed. A small farmer/miner might just fashion a random building with what he could find; the job could be part done if built in a small quarry hole, the stone floor and part of a couple of walls already in place as at a ruin at Great Longstone. (Left)

Because limestone is harder to work, on those barns the quoins, lintels, sills etc are usually made of sandstone or gritstone and again depending on the finance available these can be plain or chiselled with ornate patterns and decoration. For a large opening an arch would have to be built or a large timber beam used, as a large piece of limestone would be too heavy and brittle. Lime mortar was used as the bonding material; good for the stone work and the building as it breathes, allowing moisture to move through the walls. Being softer than cement it also makes recycling of stone much easier; in fact the majority of these barns can be and were often recycled. Ship's timbers were sometimes used in barn roofs.

Inside the cattle could be separated with a large stone boskin between a double stall and another small stone partition in between that. The beds could be earth and cobbles edged with a stone heelstone and the groop paved with stone flags and then perhaps more stone flags and cobbles outside the doorway, often specially laid to form a pathway and drainage channels. There was often a stone walled stackyard and/or stockyard too.

There might also be a stone flagged threshing floor, often in a central passageway between winnowing doors. When you consider the tons and tons of materials which had to be originally quarried, carted and dressed, and perhaps cobbles gathered from a river bed, we should really respect the work that went into these often simple looking structures. Andy Singleton in *Barns of the Yorkshire Dales* estimates there are in an average Dales barn 250 tons of materials - 180 tons rubble stone, 20 tons small rubble infill, 15 tons of stone slates, 3 or 4 tons c timber, 20 tons of flag or cobble flooring and 15 tons of corner stones, lintels etc.

The usual layout of an average barn was half earthen floored and open to the roof - the barn part, known in Yorkshire as the mow or mev - getting the hay in there could be known as 'mew hay into t' barn'. The other half was the shippon, or in North Staffordshire, 'cowuss (cowhouse). In the North of England it was known as a byre or mistal.

The stalls faced to the barn divided by a skellbuse, skellboose (Yorkshire), skelle from Old Norse - to separate. There are usually wooden racks or cratches into which the hay was put, the back of the rack often boarded to make a narrow trough to hold the hay. The stall area is known as booses (Yorks) or locally it can be boost, thought to be from the Old Norse 'bass' for stall. The bosgin or boskin, which is the partition between booses, can be made from timber, slabs of stone or latterly, formed concrete. Fixed on to the side of the boskin is an upright piece of timber or a piece of iron o steel known variously as boose-stake, ridstake, rudster or stang (all Y) or locally as rotch-stake or ratch-stake. On here was a ring which was able to run up and down known in Yorkshire as a 'framble'. To this was attached a swivel in some cases and a chain, or in the north in some places, a cowband or collar - a rope with a toggle and loop end. (See left, in Swaledale)

The bed would traditionally be earth, with perhaps cobbles and clods of earth put in to cushion the knees of the cattle. In many simple barns there was no trough as such or there may have been a simple separation with thin stones fixed on their edge. Progression could be to a flat tiled bottom or to simple, shaped concrete troughs and, where modernised, proper glazed half pipes were concreted in to make a first class trough, easy to keep clean. This was important when sheds were modernised when Tuberculin Testing came in. Wooden stallwork was usually taken out and walls rendered. The idea was that it was better able to be cleaned and disinfected. Milking cows needed more feed including concentrates and wet feeds like brewers grains and sugar beet pulp. All combined with copious amounts of cow slobber and hay seeds, so the troughs needed to be cleaned regularly; it was said a dirty trough caused mastitis and other maladies.

The muck channel is known as the groop, grip (northern dales), byre grape (east Cumbria) from Old Norse grop for drain in a cowshed. In the wall hereabouts it was common to have a small opening with a door on where muck could be shovelled through into a midden outside. There would also be various recesses in the wall to hold paraphernalia such as lamp or candles, milking tools, cattle medicines, halter, drenching bottle, cow salve, Stockholm Tar etc.

Stick loft

Above the shippon a loft kept the cattle warm. Also known as baux or baulks (Y), the singular baulk means 'a beam', and often called a stick loft because the old lofts were just branches laid over the timber beams and covered with a thick carpet of years-old hay. Many people (me included) have known the shock of your leg going through in a weak place and having to safely extricate yourself! The loft would be for extra storage for hay and in some places storage of bracken for bedding. There would generally be a couple of half-door sized openings in the upper part of the barn known as forking holes (Yorks) and locally as pitch holes, pitchin' holes or pickin holes.

A common variation of this set up is for a central feed passage with a shippon on either side with yearling stirks tied on one side and perhaps bigger stalls for heifers and dry cows on the other and a good loft over all the shed with steps outside and full sized doorway for access to the loft. The feed passage is known as fothergang, fodderbing, bing, fodderbin or fodderum.

The ironmongery would be blacksmith forged; door hinges and latches, chains, swivels, rings, gutter brackets. It was especially important to have good gutters and pipes in limestone country as every drop of water gathered from the roof was important.

Obviously an important consideration when siting a barn was where the cattle would drink. In limestone country a dewpond would have to be made if there wasn't a natural mere. In gritstone areas there was usually plenty of water in winter.

Ramped barn near Tebay

The barns were usually situated in a meadow and built to take advantage of a slope. Some are known as bank barns where the ground at the back is level with the upper floor making it easier to fill with hay. At some barns in the north of England there can even be a ramp up to large doorways. The basic idea was that hay and manure did not have to be carried far; important in hilly country with unpredictable weather and when most work was done by hand or with horses.

Like a lot of things the Second World War changed it all. Going to the outer barns was a time consuming affair depending on plenty of cheap labour which the war would quickly cause to be scarce. Horses were rapidly giving way to tractors so it was easier to cart feed and muck about and milking machines were coming in so cows had to return to the farmstead buildings to be milked. This was followed by TB eradication and capital grant schemes which drove a great increase in modern steel and concrete buildings and general modernisation which caused quite a lot of field barns to become redundant. Perhaps we are fortunate that we still have so many left and some are still being used either for sheep handling, storage or loose housing of cattle.

Other sources:
Hill Farmer by Neville Turner. 2001, Dalesman Publishing Co Ltd.
Barns of the Yorkshire Dales. Andy Singleton and David Joy, 2008 Great Northern Books.
Hay Time in the Yorkshire Dales. Various authors. 2010 Scotforth Books.
Bonsall. A Village and its History. The Bonsall History Project 2006

Rigers Barn, Leekfrith

PRACTICALITIES

Where a field barn is still in reasonable condition - that is with a roof on - they are home to owls, swallows, bats and other wildlife but before the welfare state they were often shelter for homeless people. Quite a few people still remember tramps regularly using barns to sleep in. When in use and full of livestock and hay they could be fairly snug; the only risk was fire.

was sent down to feed the cattle, worried lest someone was asleep in the hay; Congleton Bob used to be one of the tramps that regularly stayed about. They had to give you their cigarettes or pipe and matches and you gave it them back when they moved on. You might find them warming their hands on the animals and they put their coats over the cow's backs to dry.'

Some people also remember they were comfortable places for a romantic liason. An old chap related to me about one barn, 'there were more legs made there than brocken.' I will let you guess what he meant!

In our area dairy cows were usually let out on the 18th May - the young stock a week earlier. Then the clean up could start; cobwebbing and brushing down, scrubbing the bottom of the walls down and the bosgins and troughs. The bottom 3 feet of the walls were sometimes painted with tar then the top half was white-washed. This made a lighter interior and looked fresh and clean. A matter of pride was a straight line where the white-wash ended and the tar or render met.

A brush out might be all that a stirk shippon would get. Windows could be painted and doors and corrugated iron either painted or tarred. A common paint used was red oxide. On estate farms tenants were obliged to tar and paint to keep the place tidy and in good order and the estate often supplied a uniform colour of paint. The doors were left part open to let the swallows swoop in and out to their nests.

Cattle had been moved to pasture and the meadow shut up for mowing. By mid July - weather permitting - the hay crop would be ready to cut. When it was ready to carry, this often took place in the evening when it was cooler. It would be hot and sticky inside as the hay was pushed in; the day's heat radiating from the hay. The youngest helpers were stuck up in the top among the cobwebs of the roof, the hay being passed up to fill the last bit of roof space - crawling round pressing it down. All those inside waiting to hear the forks hit the bottom of the wagon then you knew the load was nearly finished.

Around the end of October the cattle were laid up. For some it would be the first time they had been tied up so help would be needed to actually tie them up the first few times. After some pulling about on their chains the first time they soon settle down and get used to a routine often returning to their own stall rather than any stall.

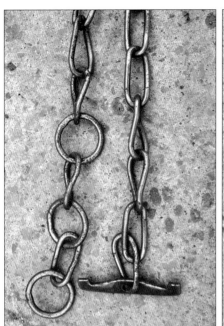

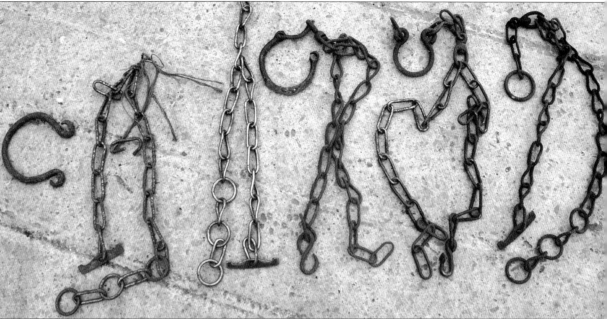

Anyone who has turned cattle out regularly will know that they a respond differently as their mates are turned out. Some wa patiently as you unfasten their chains, some dash backward before you've had chance to undo the hook and if you're no careful trap your fingers painfully in the chain so you are careful to hold onto the edges only. Old horned cows could be very craft and spin round as their chain is loosed, catching their horns in you shirt or coat and either flirt your buttons off, tear it or knock you flying. You soon get to know them and shift accordingly or where

possible loose their chains from over a bosgin.

Evidence of a more relaxed way of life waiting for the cattle to drink and come back is on the boards backing the cratches where many a lad has carved his initials and more besides; in one barn many horses are carved.

THE BARNS

Sparbent Barn, Wildboarclough

Old Wilf Massey worked on this farm in the 1920s and he used to say that another man, Noey (Noah) Holland out of 'Forest' (Macclesfield Forest) started work here as a lad and one of his jobs was to walk up to Sparbent and water the cattle. Sparbent was then run with Clough House and that was his job - good or bad weather. He was a roadman on the Cat and Fiddle for 'donkeys years' and if you saw his face he knew a bit about cold weather. He lived into his 90s.

Sparbent went with Holt in the 1930s; Rushtons were there then and it was still used for wintering cattle. There was a hydraulic ram put in with waterbowls which was still in working order when we came here. There was a fellow working for them who came from Rossendale. He took the muck with a horse and cart and a muck hook pulling it out. He was a hard man; when he got enough money together he'd go on the binge down at the Crag and I've heard people say they had found him in the gutter with water running over him next morning. He was strong as a horse then he hit the bottle and was no use for 10 days or a fortnight.

John Eardley, Clough House Farm

15

Greaves Building, Wildboarclough

A lot of these farms round here were a few acres of good land and the rest of it was moorland. Rottenstone was a typical example 14 acres near Crag Hall and then Greaves and Blubs further up Hall Lane and joining the moor. The moor that goes up to Cut Thor corner is Rottenstone Moor; it was Rottenstone Common. The 16 acres with the building in is Greaves.

The Belfield family were there for many years; they all lived in the house - Old Granny Belfield who lived into her 90s and sh had a daughter and 3 sons, none of which married. Walter was a lengthsman, Mathy - strong as a horse and Albert.

In the Greaves Building are 2 double stalls and in the end what looks like a place for pigs which could be fed from outside. I neve remember pigs but I've fed cattle there and let them out to water. But there is no storage and food has to be carried up there every day

Albert told me what a rough field it was and they wheeled 16 tons of lime out in barrows and spread it all by hand - him and hi family. There was supposed to be a sheep in the '47 blizzard as lived 26 days under the snow there.

Belfield's land was eventually put to Clough House when they got too old to farm and they stayed in the house. We had the roo taken off the building and repaired it because it is one of the oldest buildings in the Clough.   *J.E.*

16

Firs Barn, Wildboarclough

Bert Thornley was a wagon driver for the estate; he and his sister Annie lived at Firs. When I look back, if I did any work for them and had a meal there, it was a banquet and they'd be offended if you didn't have it. I was just a lad but you were looked after. They used the barn where they kept some cattle which were massive; they kept them till they were about 4 and a half years old before they sold them.

J.E.

Shutlingsloe Barn (Right)

We lived at Crag Inn Farm and my father took on Shutlingsloe Farm. The barn above the Crag Inn - we call it Shutlingsloe Barn. Ther was a shippon for 12 cows and a side shippon for calves. All tied up and let out once a day to the watering trough in the yard. Ther was a good bay for hay - we put a lot in, and a good loft. The loft was very high pitching. There was a 6 acre field there and we use to sweep the hay with a Fordson tractor to the barn then put it on a trailer to lift it onto the loft because it was that high.

When I was a lad I left school at 13 because dad had rheumatism; he was crippled. All I was interested in was farming and work. On day he sent me for a load of hay to bring from Shutlingsloe Barn down to Crag Inn with horse and cart. As the horse backed the ca into the barn to load up - it was up a bit of a slope and I was pushin' it - it slipped, its back feet went from under it and it lay down in th shafts. I didn't know what to do, being a lad; I thought, 'What'll happen now if it starts gettin' up in these shafts it'll break cart.' So I sa on its head t'hold it down and shouted and shouted for half an hour or more and nobody came. So I thought, 'Sod it, I'll get up.' I got o it's head and the horse got up and it had never broken shafts or nothin' and stood there as if nothin' had happened - so I loaded it u with hay and brought it back home. That was the end of my horse days, I said to me dad, 'I'm havin' a tractor or else I'm goin'!'

Philip Sharpley

The Crag Estate considers that field barns are an important feature of the Estate and of the local landscape. They are part of the character of the area and are wonderful examples of traditional building craftsmanship. The barns are a record of traditional farming methods, but unfortunately many of them no longer have a commercial and economically viable use. This becomes an issue when high repair costs are incurred. Some field barns have potential for conversion to other uses and this provides an incentive for maintenance. The Estate's policy towards field barns involves a careful weighing up of the relative merits of the above factors.

Big Meadow Barn

A typical barn in 22 acres; the barn in the middle of the field - ha on the loft, young stock underneath. We used it in the swee days and worked together with Philip Sharpley with a stationar wire baler until pick-up balers came in. We were banned fror using it in 1972 because they thought it was getting dangerou and it still hasn't fallen in!

J.E.

Martin Harker, land agent..

Flasker Moor Barn, Gradbach.

My Barn at Flasker Moor fascinates me because of the history around it. The first recorded mention is from 1676 when John Cooper leased 6 acres from the Brereton family. He would have to enclose it I think. There are some extraordinary stone walls just higher up.

There was a drift coal mine nearby opposite Midgely Gate and in some of the census documents Coopers' are written down as miners so I guess they would do some farming as well like so many people did in the area.

In 1803 James Shufflebotham of Flasker Moor was conscripted into the Militia at Eastborne to replace someone from Wildboarclough

In 1850 William Wain took it. It had been derelict and had been restored by the estate. (Lord Derby's)

In 1890 it was annexed to Bennettsitch. We can only assume that a cottage there had gone by then. I have had the barn since 1960; we ran sheep there and held them in the barn for shearing and worming. The roof was in a poor state and in 1995 we restored the barn with the aid of an ESA grant. I suppose it would make a nice dwelling but the trouble is when some people convert these barns they spoil them.

David Morten.

Flasker Moor.

Barn near to Winking Man.

Used to belong to Harry Gibson of School House. It was said to once have been a butcher's shop or slaughter house. Thought to be by the side of an old road from Macclesfield over to Middle Hills and Morridge.

New Meadows Barn, Swainsmoor, Upperhulme

The barn was part of a sma[ll] farm of about 20 acres whic[h] grandfather bought. We ke[pt] pigs in it and laying hens on th[e] loft. Later on we tied cattle i[n] there until 1990.

Raymond Parker

When dad bought Swainsmoor, New Meadows was a tumbledown house and barn and he had to buy that as well. We mowed the fields round it and had young stock tied there.

Father once went to feed them in wartime and there was a plane went over very low and crashed up at the side of Strines. It was a four engine bomber - a Stirling. My father was the first one there; he said there was one man still living but he died, so eight men lost their lives.

Amy Hewitt

Rigers Barn, Leekfrith

Building at Roche End

It's quite interesting because i[?] unusually built; there is [?] mortar between some of t[?] stones, it's pinned and ve[?] finely dressed. We've had mo[?] of the roof stolen.

(Datestone **PLB 1882** - Phi[?] Lancaster Brocklehurst)

The field barns have evolv[?] over time inside and out to fit [?] at the time and if possib[?] should be adapted now f[?] further use. They were practic[?] in their time; people nev[?] thought anything about walki[?] back and to because the[?] wouldn't be on £10 an ho[?] would they? It was wh[?] everybody did. *F.*

Building at Roche End

Highup Barn

Up Barn, Roches

Up Barn is on High Up Land. 36 acres called that on the deeds. It used to belong to Roche Grange. The Swythamley Estate bought it ...t 1925. They sent my granddad to the sale with an open cheque which they'd given him the night before. He said he hardly slept because ... got this signed cheque from the estate. Sir Philip wouldn't go and the agent wouldn't go because of being run up.　　　*F.B.*

...es Turner M.A. Incumbent of Meerbrook gave for ever to his ...cessors, Incumbents of Meerbrook Five Acres of Land with the Building ...eon erected, consisting of Two Bays, called Highup near Roche ...nge, for reading Prayers & Preaching a Sermon, in addition to the ...ning or Afternoon Service, on Seven alternate Sunday Evenings, ...ween the hours of 6 & 8 o'clock in the months of May, June, July & ...ust in every year. But if these Services be not performed the Rents of ...said Property are to be applied by the Trustees in purchasing Clothing, ...ls &c. To be given to poor Inhabitants of the Chapelry of Meerbrook ...very Christmas-day.　　　Enrolled in Chancery, A.D. 1845

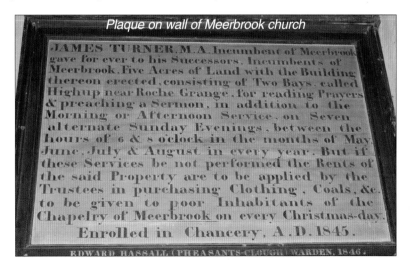

Plaque on wall of Meerbrook church

JAMES TURNER, M.A. Incumbent of Meerbrook gave for ever to his Successors, Incumbents of Meerbrook, Five Acres of Land with the Building thereon erected, consisting of Two Bays, called Highup near Roche Grange, for reading Prayers & preaching a Sermon, in addition to the Morning or Afternoon Service, on Seven alternate Sunday Evenings, between the hours of 6 & 8 o'clock in the months of May, June, July & August in every year. But if these Services be not performed the Rents of the said Property are to be applied by the Trustees in purchasing Clothing, Coals, &c. to be given to poor Inhabitants of the Chapelry of Meerbrook on every Christmas-day.

Enrolled in Chancery, A.D. 1845.

EDWARD HASSALL (PHEASANTS-CLOUGH) WARDEN, 1846.

Roche Grange Barn

Ganderhole, Quarnford. This was once a smallholding

Frank Stonier worked for us and I remember on Saturday night working at the barn down by th Meadows. The ten acre meadow was ready fo haycarting and there was only the two of us to do it. M dad was off work for some time with rheumatic feve and others were busy with their own hay. I was on fourteen and we'd had to do all the other work firs milking and everything. It was all pitchfork work and got to one o'clock in the morning; Frank was putting th hay through the pitch-hole to me and I was levelling I was so tired, I said 'I can't do any more; we'll have t leave it.' He was a strong man and his reply was 'They eether ave shift it or bloody smother in it!' What wou they say nowadays? Well, when we'd finished tha load I said 'I'm not doing any more, I just can't.' Nex day was Sunday and Dad wouldn't let us work; so had to wait till Monday and luckily the weather held

Minnie Findlow from Around Meerbrook

Pyeclough Head, Morridge Top.

New Building, Hollinsclough

The barn is known as New Building. It used to be in the middle of the Big Meadow and someone told me that it was taken down and rebuilt. On old maps it's in the middle of the meadow and there's nothing where it is now. It was used for 5 dry stock in the bottom end and 6 stirks in the top and a fodderbing up the middle with a very sloping ladder going up the far end onto the loft. The loft floor was low then you could get more hay in and it also kept the animals warmer. Father used the barn for milking in when there was Foot and Mouth and they couldn't bring the animals up the road, so they milked in there and cooled the milk in the stream.

Betty Gouldstone

Bagshaw Barn

Bagshaws lived here and they had the barn so it was known as Bagshaw Barn.

Bottom end is barn and top end were 2 shippons. A cow shippon nearest the barn and a stirk shippon as tied about 8. I can remember the estate turning it into one shippon for 8 when I were at school.

This was all rented from Crewe's until I think 1947 when Crewe's sold a lot about here and the Miss Slacks bought it. About 18 months later a tree fell on the roof of the barn. It did make a mess; it nearly broke them to fix it after buying the place.

As long as I kept a cow, I always had my hay put in there. That's why there's a fancy window; its only one piece - I can take it out and throw hay in. I brought a cow and a stirk when I fost come; a red shorthorn cow and a Guernsey stirk. That's what this place would keep so I used - before I went off anywhere - take the muck off up the field in the barrow. It's improved it no end. It took a bit of pushing up the bank then I got a little machine to take three barrowful at a time but it was so slow; you just stood on the back of it.

Henry Proctor.

Bent Barn, Near Longnor. Bent Barn stands in Jack Pasture and is accessed by Coach Lane. It was a Harpur Crewe barn. H.G.

Hollow Barn

We used to tie young stock in Hollow Barn in winter - 10 dozen. Go up there twice a day to do them - more if you had above half a mile. We once had a young Shorthorn bull up which was bad and scouring. Me and dad went up 3 times a drenching him with Jones Red Drench which was a good thing for lots of cases. He got better - we cured him.

It was all hay then - most got loose and nearly all hand w There was a loft over part of it and a barn at one end which you the hay in. Then you couldn't get it all in there and you ma stack. Hopefully you'd enough to see 'em through the winter.

We let them out down to the brook for water and after Christ we used give 'em a bit of corn to 'tice 'em back in again. If it w nice day they'd clear off and there isn't enough grass for them t You had to trust to gettin' 'em back. I can't remember much tro except perhaps in April. They'd want go and you'd let 'em i weather was alright.

If the weather was bad, it could be a problem getting there but had to walk it; your feed was there. You always made sure you spade somewhere you could get at it if you needed to dig snow a from the doors to get in.

Most barns were very dark when the doors were shut windows - just little portholes in the loft and barn end but didn't let much light in.

Harry Ge

Washgate Barn, Near Hollinsclough, by Washgate Bridge on the River Dove

...lington Farm Buildings, Longnor

...atkins used to sell hay and corn from the buildings. *RDG*

...knew these barns as Batkins Buildings in Batkins Fields because my great uncle Charlie Batkin had them. He also had a corn business ...Longnor and he used to keep fattening cattle there in those fields all summer and because he had the corn business, the corn would ...e cheaper so it was said that it was some of the best land in the area because of the good muck from the corn fed beasts.

...y father told me that Westons farmed at Village Farm, Hollinsclough in the early 1900s and they had a block of land and a barn at ...hawfield, Newtown nearly 4 miles away, up hill and down dale. One of them went and did the cattle in a morning and stayed at the barn ...ntil it was time to do them in the afternoon and then walked home. *NGM*

Cumberland Barn

At the top of the meadow Cumberland Barn is on the left and Cumberland Close on the right. They were last used for keeping stoc
in during the winter of 1968/69 when we had a fire in the farmyard and the young stock buildings were damaged. There is a waln
tree and an oak tree in the yard at Cumberland Close.

Roland Etches, Dowell Hall

Cumberland Barn

Barn at The Bank, Newtown

Dad told us that part of the barn used to be a building in the farmyard which was taken down and re-used. We put hay in it out of the meadow there; in the past we also made a stack which we cut with a hay knife and carried in - enough to last a few days - carry it up the steps and onto the loft.

One old door is made of larch and is over 100 years old because it opens inwards and Uncle Wilfred carved his name on it when he was a lad over 100 years ago. There are 'weather stones' to turn the water instead of flashing.

We last kept cattle tied in there in the winter of 2007/8. We used to keep stirks nd dry cows there - 7 stirks in one shed - and there was room for 10 in the shippon part but we rarely filled it. We'd go down in he morning after milking in the yard and fodder them, then again later to let them out to drink at the brook and go down at night to odder them again.

Ve put water bowls in after 1963 when it froze the brook every day - the only time we knew of it doing that. We had an old axe to hop out the ice so they could get to the water underneath. Then it was too cold for them to drink much. We had to carry water to hem sometimes.

: was always a job getting there to do them in a blizzard. We had to rid a way through the snow down to the brook at times and we'd huck hay seeds down to make the way look black so they'd follow it better.   *R and NW*

Frost Building

The barn at Fawfieldhead we called Frost Building. There are some fields there called Frost Meadow and Frost Pasture. When I left school and we tied cows up at backend, we used take a few over there as were goin' dry and I used go with a bucket and stool and milk 'em once a day and I've been and milked 4 cows and come back with a gallon and half of milk - but it all counted.

There was water down the field - two places as never went dry which they were let out to. Then my dad and a lad called John Harrop dug all the way - about 400 yards - from the top building near the roadside to there - dug it in about 2 foot deep. Skinners came and it was all done with galvanised pipes screwed together. It was fed by gravity so we put water bowls in.

1958 was a bad summer and we never finished the hay completely that year. We mowed 2 swathes across the bottom side of a field there so that we could mow into the lie of the grass and we carted it by hand - me and me dad, 2 swathes a day. The swathe was that matted, you had to roll a bit one way then roll a bit th'other way, then pick it up and load it onto the cart. We made a grass stack and poured black treacle on it out of a watering can and then we 'pulled' it like a haystack. We called it a 'salvage stack'; it was good stuff considering it was made in October - the outsides were bad of course. It was heavy work again, cutting it and carrying it in with a fork to the cows in winter.

John Mellor

Barn at Waterhouse Farm.

Barn at Waterhouse Farm

All of our barns were Harpur Crewe barns; I think it was about 1923 when the farm was bought from the estate. The big barn, we know as 'over at barn'. In one part, on the right were the calves and on the left, a stage bigger. In the top end, that was always the heifer shippon they were bigger still. Then the fodderbing, where there are all names carved in the wood.

The water trough is on the little yard. Uncle Robert went to let them out; he was gone from 11 till 1 o'clock and would have them all out maybe 3 at once. When he got as he couldn't do it, I had to do it before I took the children to school.

We put hay on the loft from the 2 meadows there and if there was more than it could hold we made a haystack round the back. Father thatched the stack with straw; he could do it ever so nice. I remember Sep and Jim from Boothlow fetching rushes for thatching from Boars Grove and coming back with a great big load. They'd be gone all day.

The barn hasn't been used for 25 years.

Mary Boam

Windy Arbour Barn

Windy Arbour Barn is in Windy Arbour Ground. My father used to milk in there; batch milking in the summer when the cows were grazing on that land. He used to cool the milk in a small stream behind the barn then he would take it with his horse and trap to the Cheese Factory at Glutton Bridge. He milked there until the late 1950s. A friend of his used to work on the neighbouring farm and would call in on his way home from work.

Dad would be hand milking the cows and would say 'Are you going to give us a hand to finish milking?' and his friend used to say 'If you haven't finished next time I come past, I'm carrying on; I'm not having this every night'   *Richard Gould*

Windy Arbour Barn

Windy Arbour Barn

Town Field Barn   Stiff Close, Longnor

We refer to it as the Building Field. We no longer tie cows up in there; we have put cubicles in. We still find it useful to have stock in there in the winter; it takes about half an hour a day to look after them. We just need to make sure that we can fill the loft with hay in the summer, as there is no stone track across to the building and the fields get too wet to get near with a tractor.

Richard Gould

Town Field Barn

Town Field Barn

Herbage Barn, Warslow Moor

When we bought The Herbage, the barn had got wooden boskins in and a loft made out of branches. It was all taken out and we put a concrete floor in it and from then had it for running sheep in and sorting sheep from lambs.

Old Colin, the tramp - he went in a part of it all through one winter. When the sheep weren't up there, we didn't go in so when spring came and we went up to get the sheep in, we were as shocked as he was. He jumped up and went outside, did about 4 circles because he was that taken to, then went off up the road. He didn't come back again because he thought we were using it. We had to clean all these bottles and tin cans up. He'd got all the holes in the wall packed up with paper to keep the draught out. Now the barn isn't used at all unless the army shelter in it while they are training up there.

Reg Day

Left: Colin
Photographer unknown

Warslow Moors Estate

The Warslow Moors Estate was acquired by the PDNPA in 1986 from the government in lieu of tax owed by the previous owners, the Harpur-Crewe family. The estate amounts to nearly 5,000 acres of moorland, rough grazing, meadow and pasture and woodland. There are about 35 field barns in various conditions from derelict to excellent and our policy has been to score ones that need action against various criteria with the three possible outcomes

. Fully restore and try and find a viable use

. Moth ball by tidying up, storing materials and capping to keep the water out of the walls in the hope that funds will
   be available to restore in the future

. Record with photos and measurements but demolish leaving footings

There are about 10 barns that fall into the first category. We have tried to make progress with them through the Higher Level Stewardship Scheme traditional building restoration grant at 80% but the funding now seems to have ceased for anything that is not exceptional in architectural terms.

The problems are that they are not much or any use for modern farming, difficult to get planning on for alternative uses and cost round £20,000 each to restore depending on condition. However they are obviously an integral part of the cultural heritage and landscape and therefore clearly within our policy to maintain them where at all practical.   *Chris Manby, Estates' Manager*

Old Ralphs Barn, Reapsmoor

Billy Prince used to milk in Old Ralphs Barn. We took it on when we farmed Knowle House Farm and kept dry cows and youn
cattle in it. The farm belonged to the Harpur Crewe estate. They were good landlords; we got on well with the agent, Mis
Claudia Severn.

Henry and Marjorie Mycock.

op Barn, Steps Farm, Warslow

)ur barn we call Top Barn. We tied 4 heifers in it. The hay barn was right to t' floor and you had your cutting knife and cut your
/ay in to front o' t' cratches. When weather were bad we never let 'em out; you'd go to t' brook with couple o' buckets for water.
Ve had dig to 'em when snow come and snow was high as mantelpiece (5 feet) to get to t' brook. We used whitewash it every
ear; it makes it lighter and keeps it clean.

   We had one horse - did all - went with milk every day in a float - come back - mowed - carted. There was a lot o' hard work;
e used have ted by hand wi' a fork. A bloke out o' Longnor used buy these horses out o' Manchester that had been on these
rays. The last one was a pure shire off somebody at Dove Holes. Best horse we ever had. We called 'er Phyllis and she'd come
 us but they said they called her Bonny!

   All these buildings were used; many people out o' Warslow milked at these barns and used take the milk to their lane end on
 trolley and fetch empty churn back. The milk stands are still there. When Uncle Tom went to Hayes in 1945 nobody wanted the
arms because there were no electric or anything. He had the barn that goes with Hayes Cottage and milked in it and when TT
ɔb came in, George Wain who worked for Harper Crewe did it up for him with a loose box in one end, concrete troughs and high
tandings.

Cliff Gould

Top Barn

Top Barn, November Haymaking

Hayes

Hayes, Warslow.

ld Building, Reapsmoor

t Reapsmoor the first barn belonged to Spout Farm. We call it the Old Building. The next barn is called the Arbour because a bloke
alled Billy Arbour lived in it. Old Ellens is further up; there is a fire place in the top end. Me grand mother could remember it being
ccupied in the 1890s. It's been in the Lomas family for generations.

I remember my uncle at Field House keeping dry cows in the barns. He swapped them round for cows that were milking. Used
I three barns; trek round 'em all. I used clean 'em out, feed 'em and took 'em water in. There was a trough outside and I used
arry buckets of water in. At the Old Building we let 'em out to a trough in the Acre Field. When they'd drunk they'd come back in.
There is Old Building Meadow, Old Ellen's Front and Back Fields, Old Ellen's Pasture, Back of Big Wall Field. Folly Field is farthest
ne away and Heathy Field was all over short heather when Grandad first took it on - No-Mans Land and they took it in and put a
nce round it. Granddad moved a wall and took more in; the Butchers Arms did the same thing. Crewe and Harpur came and said,
ook, you're taking our ground. If you don't move the wall we'll sue you for claiming land that isn't yours.' So them at Butchers
rms moved their wall back but my granddad didner do and he never heard no more about it.   *David Lomas*

The Arbour

Old Ellens

The Barn, Crow Trees Farm, Lower Elkstone

We used keep young stock in it, just called it The Barn. Me dad said they used hand- thresh corn in theer at one time becaus
there's one door at back and one opposite at front. They used take sheaves in and thresh it by hand so it blew all chaff out an
left corn in. Me granddad did it during wartime. It was a wet time and they had mow it all by hand and he threshed it in theer bes
he could.

David Lomas

Barn on the Om

On Ecton Hill, the land from the 'castle' towards Dale Farm we knew as the Om. Before my time Mr Naylor from Ecton Lee was gamekeeper at Swainsley and I believe he kept some cattle up in that barn on the Om.

Nancy Coates

Bassetts rented the Om from Lady Gaunt of Swainsley Hall. John Bassett of Cawlow told me someone used go with horse and trap and milk at the barn up there. (Mr Naylor of Ecton Lee) It's all grown over now where they used to go up the hill. *Bill Mellor*

Butts Barn

We used to put stirks in. It held 2 in the little shed and ... in the bigger shed and then there was the hay barn. We'd go across and water them from the trough below. They ought to have put a fence down to stop ...em running about; I don't know why they didn't. When you turned them out the first day cousin Tom ...om Low End had to come and help get them in.

Our bottom barn is known as Uncle John's Barn. My ...ister and I did the cattle; I'd go to the top barn (Butts) ...nd she'd go to the bottom and the ones as did the ...est, dad said he'd treat us but we never got nothin, ...e said they'd both done the same. They were sent to ...rink at a small rindlet. We put big double doors in ...ne end later and kept the haytime machines down ...here. *Hilda Critchlow*

Ashulme Barn - part of the Warslow Hall Estate

Our folks lived in a house there. On a will of Peter Mellor dated 1807 it is spelt Ash Holmn. The Harpur Crewes at Warslow Hall decided they didn't want to be overlooked so the estate sent Mrs Mellor to Manor Farm, Hayes Gate and then knocked the house down.

Bill Mellor

Engine House Barn

Dick and William Henry Bonsall from Westside had the Fishpond Barn - it was their ground. In winter we used to see William Henry come down from Westside with a sack crammed full of hay stuck on the end of a hay fork over his shoulder to feed the stirks. He always said he was glad when the time came as it was still daylight at 5 o'clock and he could see to feed them better.

We had the Engine House Barn. We had cattle tied in it - young stock; 4 bigger ones tied one way and 5 smaller ones the other way with stone bosgins in between them. You'd go up twice a day, sometimes 3 times - even in bad weather and it *was* bleak up there.

They were watered at a mere down in the ground. When it was frosty we had a crowbar there and you had to knock a hole in the ice for a start so they could drink. Sometimes it was blizzarding we used to carry snow in because they wouldn't face it - going out into the blizzard. They'd just stand there with their heads down so we put some snow in front of them so they could lick it. There was other water in the plantation - that comes out of the Dutchman Mine. The there was catch water.

You let them out, cleaned out and put the feed in, then they'd come back. The groop was very narrow and you got black leg a time or two if you got kicked.

To get on the loft you climbed up a plank with toe holes in. In summer we used to back up to the little pitch hole with the horse and cart and unload the hay through it then push down into the barn part. We couldn't use the front door because that led onto the shaft which was open then with a high wall round it.

One day up there Jim slipped on some ice and broke his ankle. He had to come down the hill on his bottom then pulled a stick out of the hedge to get home with. He wore a balaclava; it used to have icicles on.

Swallows always nested in there; when spring came you always had to have the pitchin' holes open. *Nancy Coates*

This used to be the engine house to Ecton Copper Mine. It ceased to be used for mining around 1891 and became a field barn. In 1930 the second storey was removed and the roof relaid.

Littler Barn, Warslow

I've worked here for over 60 years. Years ago we used milk down there - used go down early in a morning with a lantern with a candle in it and sometimes it would blow the candle out and you had start again. Used carry milk up into the yard. Jimmy Philips worked here as well; he used wear clogs and went in shippon one morning, slipped on his back and hit his head on the concrete. We stopped milking down there when Jimmy finished and kept young stock and dry uns down there.

Don Wooliscroft

The Engine House Barn can be seen on the left sky line.

Littler Barn

Shepherds Barn, Moorside, Warslow

SOME BARN INTERIORS

Bottom Barn, Berresford Dale Lane

ottom Barn, Cross Farm, Sheen

t weekends and school holidays I used to go and help John Shann at Cross Farm. We used to go twice a day and let the cattle out om the barn for water which at that time was a pond which was half in the field and half on the roadside divided by a wall. It was bout 20 yards long and 5 yards each side; I suppose it was the village pond and it had tadpoles and frogs in. It's all gone now.

When you opened the barn door you had to be prepared to find a tramp asleep on the hay in the middle. It was a warm place r them in winter. One we knew as Nobby.

The cattle came back in readily because we had put feed in their troughs; a mixture of chopped mangolds or turnips, chopped traw and brewers grains.

I helped John and his dad with the haymaking; gathering the loose hay and forking it through the pickin hole and I remember rank Moorcroft used to come and shoot rooks in the trees at the vicarage and we ent round to pick them up and then Mrs Shann used to make Rook Pie.

Arthur Howson

Je understand that the original barn was by the mere and when it was rebuilt further way they put the original datestone back in and a new datestone below it. Great randad Shann carved the horses on the cratches inside; they said the cattle had go farther to get water when the mere dried up so he did it while waiting for them come back. When Deep Lane was widened the spoil was used to fill the mere in.

Herbert Shann

Calf Cote, Butterton

We used have heifers and stirks across there; it tied 11 of various sizes from big calves to bulling heifers. We let them out t Coppitt Pond, a stone dewpond once a day. It's not been used for 25 years.

Peter Gibbs

Townlow Barn, Butterton

Townlow Barn is situated next to Townlow - a Neolithic burial ground. It's unusual as unlike most other tumuli in the area it has not been excavated. When my husband's parents married in the 1940s they took over that part of the farm and used the barn to house and milk their cows. They would take a horse and cart, churns and their baby daughter and a picnic and have tea over there. It's such a beautiful spot- my mother in law used to say it was one of the happiest times of her life.

I was once sent to Sand Meadow Barn to clean out the fodderbing. I stuck my fork in what I thought was a pile of old hay and a huge badger rushed out from underneath and nearly knocked me over.

We have two barns which have been converted to camping barns. Waterslacks barn was the cattle byre for Waterslacks Farm but is now part of Broadmeadows Farm. The other camping barn is Wills Barn set in Wills field probably named after William Hambleton the local squire who owned many of the farms in the area including Wall Acre, Broadmeadows and Lane House Farm.   *MR*

Sand Meadow Barn

Deepdale Farm Outer Barn. Grindon

When I was young I used to go and do the cattle for my uncle and they had to go all the way down the steep hill to water troughs which were fed by a spring. They also grew a few potatoes in a slang up there; I remember getting them.

My dad used to say, 'I'll swape thraowin' off.' That was the back of the bed of the stall. The front could be made of clods so was soft for them to lie on and I think the bosgin stake could be called a thrampit.

The little barn is known as Porch Farm Barn because it used to go with Porch Farm.

My uncle, William Simpson of Onecote told me that in the 1947 winter Mester Wood of Slade House found his cattle dead their chains in the barn because he couldn't get to them. He added 'If he'd a loosed 'em an' left dooer oppen they wouldn't dayd.' The weather was that bad he couldn't face it; he would have been cast away.

Brian Simpson

Porch Farm Barn

Arborton Barn, Gateham Grange

Arborton Barn is on Arborton Land. On a map dated 1922 Mr Adams had called it Top Barn and there are 2 fields up there marke 'flints found'. We know that land as Flints. The Adams would have kept young stock up there and there are the remains of a mer in front of the barn.

There are the ruins of a barn to the west of Narrowdale Hill which on the same map is marked Winnyatts. Mrs Adams told us used to be Wineyards.

We also have a barn on the east of Narrowdale Hill called Butterlands Barn. We have converted it to a camping barn an managed to incorporate the hayracks as features. There is no electricity to the barn; just a water supply. It is a successful ventur and we are pleased with it.

Robert Flower

Arborton Barn

Old Building, Gateham

The Old Building at Gateham

We put stirks and dry cows in. They were watered at a mere; we hadn't an ounce of running water so had to preserve all the mere - we had several down Long Lane. Some have been filled in now. You kept them cleared then, you'd got to and we caught all th roof water.

   The barn hasn't been used for a good many years. These barns were used when people worked for next to nothing - you couldn justify the time now for a few cattle.

FY

Barn, Gateham

Gratton Barn, Green Farm, Alstonefield

In my mum and dad's day in the 1940s we milked outside in the yard in summer; it saved bringing the cows down the road t the farmyard and wearing their feet. There was mum, dad, me and my sister Ruby and anyone who worked for dad at the tim We just went up to them with stool and bucket and while you were milking, if one was in service you might get a foot on top c your head.

We took churns and sie dish up with a little Ferguson and transport box and brought the milk home to cool it in a big tank of wate pumped from a large cistern in front of the farmhouse.

In winter the barn tied 16 stirks and dry cows. They were let out to a pond which you had to dig out of the snow to find. In a lon winter it would get lower and lower.

We turned out on 12th May and then there was a job I hated - white washing. There was no water to scrub out with so we ha to scraper the muck off the walls and cobweb then whitewash round halfway down. I didn't mind the scraping but didn't like gettin lime in my eyes! There used to be a thrashing floor at one time - wooden planks which have now rotted. *Marjorie Mycock*

Photos courtesy of Tim Eades,
Alstonefield Memories

CLOCKWISE

Alf Petts Snr at Damgate

James Bailey of Hope Mount

James Bailey with churn wheels

Herbert Allen on Millway Lane 1947

Slipperlow Barn, and opposite page

Wetton Barns

The barn above Thors Cave is known as Thurses Building. Thurses Farm is in the village and Ken Thompson was there. He ha a building in the village and three fields - he hadn't a lot of land. It was all belonging to Chatsworth and when he packed up it wa all put to other farms. They were good landlords.

He milked down Thurses Building in summertime and fetched the milk back by tractor and before that by horse and cart. In winte it was used for tying young cattle. All the farmers milked outside in summer; they weren't big herds then. People used to go out o the land to where the cows were and go up to them with bucket and stool and the cow would stand there while it was milked. The stood without corn; they got used to it. I did it till the 50s then farmers started having milking machines so it meant the cows ha to come home to the buildings. We all used to go - mother, father, sister, brother with tractor and trailer, empty churns, sie dis buckets, stools. We'd ground at different areas - it depended where the cows were grazing; when they'd eaten the land you move them. We'd a piece of land and a building going down to Hope Dale - Nether Barn. You could be sat there in the field in pourir rain with water running off the cows into the bucket; it was different to today - they weren't as particular.

Slippler Barn (Slipperlow), Stubbs' had it. They didn't milk in there but used to go and milk in the land. They'd bring them down the side of the road.

John Wint

Nether Barn, Wetton, October 2010, restored by Chatsworth Estate

Sad story of arson April 2011

Nether Barn in December 2005 before restoration

Eccles Tor Barn, Grove Farm, Stanshope

This building was used up until about 20 years ago. The stock were all wintered on the land and ran in and out freely. My parents Tom and Zena had stirks tied up which they had to walk up to a dew pond a field and a half away. I've heard my Dad say that he had to dig through 3 feet of snow and cut through a foot of ice to enable them to have a drink.

We made little bale hay of the surrounding fields which were stacked in this barn. Billy Glanville, the local water bailiff who lived at Lode Mill used to come and help at hay time and bring with him an ex-army 'champ' which was an American jeep. We used this to cart the hay.

Another character was Billy Higton. He would tell us the story of how he was in the army on the front line when a bullet went through his braces and let his trousers down.

Nick Bonsall

Barn at Thorpe Mill Farm, Ilam

Barn at Ilam Tops Farm

The barn belongs to Ilam Tops Farm which used to belong to the Hanbury Estate centred on Ilam Hall. Dad came here in 1943. There was tying for 10 dry cows and 6 yearlings and a stable on the end which was converted to a loose box. There was a mere close by but when that got too dirty there was a clean one on top of the hill. Dad said in February 1962 there was a terrible gale and he wished he had a camera when the cattle went up to the top mere, they were walking at a forty-five degree angle. We still use the barn.

Jim Burton

Barns at Sharplow Farm, Tissington.

The square barn we know as Washbroo Barn. It is in a field on the map known a Westbrook Pingle.

The barn behind is Barn in Jimmy's Field.

Michael Stubbs

The farm used to belong to the Tissington Estate

84

Tissington Barns

As a child I lived at the lodge at the Avenue Gates at Tissington. Birches farmed from the blacksmiths shop in the village where old Mr Birch was the blacksmith. The farm was split into three; they kept calves and young stock in the Avenue Barn where two tramps used to sleep on the hay on the loft, one more often than the other. Mum always said, 'Keep away from them.'

I used to go with Birches in the horse and cart up to Moor Barn; that looks straight down into Dovedale - it's fantastic up there. There's many barns that have disappeared; there was a beautiful barn on Hollington for horses - on the highest point. I can remember shire horses which belonged to the estate being kept in that; my granddad was waggoner at the hall. Ducks Nest Barn was another beautiful barn now gone down by Mill Pond Planting.

Another barn was Butchers Barn; I used to feed cattle there in the 40s and 50s. It went with Wibben Hill Farm. There were four great big cesterns (cisterns) for the water (from the roof). When it ran out we carted it with tractor and churns. There were Butchers fields there - two fields which went with the butchers shop and opposite Green Farm another field which is now part of the village playing field. When they bought the livestock from Ashbourne, Leek, Uttoxeter and Bakewell markets they put them in there until they wanted to slaughter them.

Past Butchers Barn was Grewy Ditch Barn which is now gone. It was a lovely square barn with a pointed roof; it was unusual. Old Dick Torr used to build a hayrick there and make a fantastic job of thatching it.

On the Flatts was a tiny barn which we called Johnsons Barn which Chris Carr knows as Pingle Barn. We used to play 'Fox and Hounds' when we were at school with all these barns. One of you ran off - he was the fox - and hid. We used to play it at dinner time at school; we used to be late back and say, 'he's hiding in Johnsons Barn.'

Then there's Grannys Little Barn. Wilfred Smith had it; they kept calves in it. On the door were various initials carved - perhaps courting couples. We tried to work them out - JB loves.... There was a lovely old iron bridge over the railway nearby for the footpath to Parwich. This would come after the barn and was known as Grannys Bridge. One day in the 70s we heard this bang and the Peak Park had blown the bridge up.

Les Alcock

Avenue Barn

My dad, Jack Carr used go to the Hiring Fair at Ashbourne and he went to various farms; they were hired for 12 months. In 1909 h went to the fair and he was set on by George Johnson of Overfield Farm, Tissington to start on the 1st January 1910. From then c he made his home with them for the rest of his life.

The barn that stands in Town Meadow goes with Overfield and during the wintertime there were 21 young stock tied up in sing standings. Mr Johnson used go down every morning and let them drink at the Bletch Brook while he cleaned them out and foddere them. There was a little yard round the back which they'd made a rick in. He had to cut the hay loose and feed it. Meanwhile da was on the farm up here; they milked about 30 by hand with bucket and stool.

Pingle Barn: To look at it, it appears to be dry-stone walling but there is mortar in the middle of the stones. There is only one other like that which I know of in the village and that is First Croft Barn. Next to Pingle Barn was a separate field of half of an acre. There's a bank goes down there even now. It belonged to the estate in the 1950s in Sir William Fitzherbert's time. Mr Johnson asked the agent if they would sell it because it was right down the centre of Town Head. The estate were reluctant to sell it but eventually the agent, Colonel Wheatman came and said, 'Sir William is willing to sell the Pingle but its got that barn on it you know and he thinks it ought to be £100.' 'Right - Done!' said Mr J, though it was quite a lot of money in the 1950s. I was working on the farm then, so we took the hedge out.

Avenue Paddock Barn We call it 5 (next to the A road). It has high mange so may have been for horses. Th wooden corn bin (below) was there whe we took over; it's tin lined to keep verm out. If a part of a barn had an open fro we tended to call it a cart hovel; yc could back a cart in. Raikes Lane Bar is now a glass studio. *Chris Car*

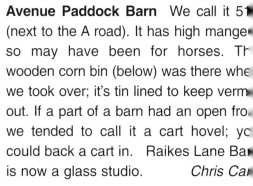

own Meadow Barn

Ve use Town Meadow building for catching stock - sheep and cattle at worming times and that sort of thing;
s hard work trying to capture your cows in the middle of nowhere. We see little owls and tawny owls in
ere. The building is well built and in quite good order and worth maintaining for what we do with it.

hapel Barn, Brookwood

Ve had hens in it and cattle. It was sad to see it drop to pieces because it seemed historic; there were
ads of fossils in the stones. When we had hens in there sometimes rats would come in taking eggs so
other would shoot them with a 4.10 shotgun and sometimes kill the odd hen with a stray pellet. *Tony Stone*

Barn at Shaws Farm, Tissington

was lucky enough to inherit the two and a half thousand acre estate of Tissington in 1989 and I have lived here and managed it for 24 years. On our estate are between 20 and 30 outlying barns. Some are used, some not and they need a new life or some appreciation or we shall lose them. We have already lost some for repairs on other buildings or farmsteads on the estate.

Just looking around at some of the barns in the Peak District it seems we have a heck of a resource of barns, some of which are loved and cared for and fully utilised and others not. I think here in the 21st century we need to be looking at other ways to utilise them or we are going to lose them to the landscape. At Tissington we have tried to work with the planners and the National Park in order to do this. I have saved 2 or 3 but there are another 10 or 12 that are in dire straits which I would like to do something with but there is little grant aid that I can find.

The other interesting point is that not all the barns have Staffordshire blue tiles on their roofs; some keep the rain out with wonderful stone slabs that were quarried locally in often small family-farm quarries. Nowadays there are far fewer of these sorts of quarries existing (if any at all) and it is more and more difficult and expensive to obtain repair material.

Grannys Little Barn, also known as Finny Ground Barn.

Barn at Shaws Farm

Raikes Lane Barn

I have been fortunate enough to have inherited these wonderful barns on the Tissington Estate. Some of them have new lives as holiday cottages or craft barns but I desperately hope that we can save the others with vernacular appreciation and an 'evolution' approach to their future use.

Sir Richard FitzHerbert Bt

Moor Barn - used to belong to Tissington Estate

Moor Barn was and still is used for lambing. Part of the building we call the cabin where you can sleep and there is a fireplace with ovens where they could warm lambs up. The sheep were shut in the crofts and brought into sheds as they lambed. There used to be a low tin shed and a fair garden.

Next to the cabin was where they tied shire horses with sandstone ends to the bosgins and 2 foal standings behind.

There was a bull shed in the corner and a tying shed for 8 with a bing but small standings. A little shed at the top tied 6 calves. There is a loft over both sides with a central corn place, wooden floored, a foot off the ground. The brick shed is a later building.

All Dovedale - the 7-800 acres would be linked to Moor Barn - and what I know as Sharpler Dale (Sharplow) went with Sharplo and had a big timber building on it. There is also Back Moors - 80 acres which would join Face Moor buildings.

When granddad and then dad took Moor Barn we kept Dovedale to the Stepping Stones and up to Tissington Spires and the Sharpler Dale and when I left school we took Nabs Dale on - down the back of Hanson Grange and now I've taken Back Moor or It's all owned now by the National Trust.

David Torr.

Gone from Tissington. Two on left, Sawpit Bank Barns. Right, Narlow Lane Barn (courtesy Chris Carr)

Fleets Barn, New Hanson Grange

Fleets Barn, New Hanson Grange

In land called Fleets which was part of the Alsop estate which was sold in 1919. In the 1960s we had 10 heifers tied in there whic' were let out to the mere to drink. The mere was filled from the road. We mowed those fields and filled the loft with hay bales an brought the rest home. When it ran short you took some more bales down. It was walled round where the planting is. It could hav been a stackyard years ago; that's what was usually at the back of the building - it was where they built a stack in the old days.

Tom Bunting

Barn at Moatlow Farm, Newton Grange

Little Barn, Bletch Brook area, Parwich

Bill Austin would use it. He would have a haystack and it tied 4 with a bing at the front.

Charles Bunting

95

arn at Oxdale Farm, Alsop Moor

he barn was owned by ICI along with a piece of land around it. They had the Alsop Moor Quarry next to it and dad had the barn
nt free because sometimes during blasting you'd get a shower of rocks which damaged the building. He used to keep young
tock up there. It was last used in the 1950s when TB testing came in. The reactors were kept up there and dad went up twice a
ay to hand milk them.

Mark and Peter Edge

Harrocks Barn, Hartington. Also known as Harrods and on an Ordnance Survey, Harrots.

Barn to Digmer Farm, Hartington

The barn stands in Barn Meadow; when I was a kid, dad tied 5 stirks in it and had loose hay on the loft. I remember going up with him; they were loosed out to a nearby mere and there was also a stack of hay in the bottom near Harrocks Barn. I understand that name came from 'Hare Rocks'. John and George Mellor and their dad, John Peter from Moat Hall had it. In the 60s I used to go up with John every day on the tractor; I did the gates so he didn't have to get off and then I'd go and feed my stock up there while he did his.

Peter Birch

Below, Harrocks Barn with Barn to Digmer Farm on far right.

On Highfield Lane, Hartington

Hills Barn, Reynards Lane, Hartington

Staden Barn, Hartington

Staden Barns, Hartington

Called Staden Barn from a man called Staden who owned the land in the1800s. We still use them for livestock. The little barn ha
ship timbers in it.

Morson Family

...arns, Crossland Sides (Centre, with Staden Barns in foreground)

...e milked 42 cows at what we call John Willys Barn (Crossland Sides) at Hartington - Me, dad and Uncles Ralph and Leopold. ...e milked with units and churns. We made hay up at Timothy Barn on Hide Lane and then when the aftermath was ready we ...alked the cows up and milked them up there at the barn, ten at a time with an old David Brown tractor and a belt driven vacuum ...ump. That was until milk tankers came in and they wouldn't pick up milk from John Willys Barn.

Ralph Bassett

Timothy Barn, Hide Lane, Hartington

Hardings Barn, on Harding Gap Lane, Hartington

Booths Barn, Biggin

Used to go with Biggin Grange. Dating from late 18th century to early19th century and restored by the National Trust. In the background, left is Ferny Bottom Barn, and right is Hills Barn.

Grindlow Barn, near Sheldon

Great grandfather, James Frost, owned the land where Greenlow Building and True Blue Barn are. He built the barns in the 1890s True Blue cost £60 and Greenlow £100. He left the land split between his 2 sons - Herbert William, my grandfather and John Fros My dad used to tie cows in True Blue; it held eight. I do remember as a child, walking across there with him; I thought it was a lon traipse. A nice building though.

Grandfather was at the Bobbin Mill and came to Manor Farm, Sheldon in 1900, renting it from Chatsworth. He bought that piece of ground known as Grindlow and the barn in the early 1920s - 35 acres for £570. He was a dealer in cattle; he bought a lot of cattl in springtime from up north and sold them off during the year. There could be up to 300 and they were chiefly Shorthorns

John Frost

Greenlow Building, near Sheldon

True Blue Barn

We have True Blue Land and True Blue Barn and the lane between there and Greenlow Building is True Blue Lane. Dad said was called that because in the lead mine there, they found a vein of blue stone. There is a winding circle which has a protectio order on it - we don't do anything there - and a good mere. That land of the Frosts' was some of the only land in the area whic didn't belong to Chatsworth a hundred years ago. Slates have been stolen from the roofs - that was the end of Tomlinson's bar next to Magpie Mine when that roof was stolen.

Bernard Frost

Willow Shallows Barn, Monyash.

had a blue slate roof which was stolen 20 years ago.

George Cantrell

Bakewell Barns

From a high point on our land a few years ago I counted about 20 of these small field barns dotted around this area. There were lots of small farms and people got a living by mining or quarrying and a bit of farming; they couldn't get a living out of either on its own. Lead mining was very much an industry in the 1800s in this part of the world and a chert mine goes under our land here or they could go into a limestone quarry and it was all a very hazardous affair.

Livestock would be kept on the ground floor of the barns and someone could live or sleep in the bothy upstairs. In my view the barns should be maintained either by grant or such planning so that people can have an income to maintain the barns themselves; it can't be done out of love!

Ian Lawton

urst Building, near Ashford

he roadside building is known as Hurst Building. It stands in Hurst Field. It would be run by a family living in Ashford.

he little barn stands in Boots Land, a 55 acre block which used to belong to Mr Boot who was at Thornbridge Hall in the 1930s.
ve always known it as a cattle shelter. There was also Big Boots Building which is now fairly ruined. A gritstone channel runs from
ere which filled a mere.

Brian Greenhalgh

Little Barn in Boots Land

Dutch Barn, Little Longstone

My grandfather, Isaac Shimwell died in 1960 in his 85th year. He told me about the barn known as Dutch Barn. It was a grand Shepherds Barn for lambing and he could remember it being used as such. The sheep were folded on the enclosed yard and used the bottom of the barn and the fodder was stored above. In one end of the loft was the bothy with fire place and chimney. There would be a mere in front of the yard.
John Shimwell

We call it 'Cathedral Barn'; it belongs to Little Longstone Estate and the Longsdon family. It is grade 2 listed. *James Longsdon*

hapel Building at ittle Longstone.

Make Leas Field. It was run from ong Roods Farm by Ben and Willie himwell for stirks and storage for ay. There was a mere at the top of e field now filled in. We run sheep it in winter.

iranddad Isaac Shimwell had an ishman for harvesting. He'd work r so many days then go to lonsall Head Hotel and get drunk r a day or two. *David Neal*

The Building Under the Moor, Great Longstone

In wintertime they kept dry cows u[...]
there, tied up. There were 2 sheds [...]
one held 10 and one 6. When th[...]
cows to go dry got onto once a da[...]
milking they took them up there an[...]
George Redfern who worked for u[...]
would go up there and feed them, l[...]
them out to the pond, fill th[...]
cratches up with hay then tie ther[...]
up and milk these once a day cow[...]
in a bucket and carry the milk back[...]
It must be half a mile or more.

Small barn in 'Grisedale', nearb[...]

George worked here for 50 years and he only had one day off. He felt unwell but they were busy so asked him at dinner time if he could come back; which he did. He told me he once drove some cows to Bakewell Market and went to the dentist where he had all his teeth out but as my father had bought some cattle he helped to drive them back. He said, 'All the way back I was spitting blood.' He was a hard little chap; he knew not the first thing about machinery but was dedicated to animals.

When there were more buildings at the farm we used to keep hens in the barn; about 3-4 hundred free range. George used to walk up and let the hens out and walk back down again carrying all the eggs in buckets, perhaps 100 eggs in each bucket. I used to remember when the hens were let out they used to run down to the pond for a drink - there was a ring of probably 200 hens having a drink out of the pond. *Ian Cox*

oolow Barns

here are several substantial barns around Foolow which are built in a similar style by the Wyatts who owned Watergrove Mine. hey bought land in and around the village, and I believe these barns would be built around the time of enclosure there in1804. ne of the barns - Willowbeds - was converted to a house around 1904.

Richard Eastwood

This barn used to be a little cottage where George Maltby lived; he was a lead miner at Magpie Mine and had a colourful past being involved in a dispute with Red Soil Mine close by it. In 1834 this resulted in him along with 17 others being charged with murder but then acquitted.

Perhaps because of this he became a leader among local Methodists and is famous for composing the music for one of the Foolow Carols called Marshall. This is sung outside here very Christmas as the carol singers go round the village.

Paradise Farm, Bradwell

I was four when my grandparents moved here from Cotes Farm which was taken for the quarry. My granny's family owned the farms. We have four field barns and I remember we used to look in the ventilation holes for pigeons. I was betrayed as a child - Grandad sent me up on the baulks at Maltby Tops one time. 'If you look in the window,' he said 'there's a pigeon's nest there.' I went, full of joy. 'Aren't they pretty,' he said, 'Just pass one down for me to look at.' So I passed it down. 'Well, let me see the next one.' That one disappeared as well - only to reappear the next day in pigeon pie! Granny and Grandad were rather fond of it. Grandad went down a bit in my estimation.

Muck door

The Top Barn is a big barn. The shippon part has wooden floors in the standings like sleepers and if the cows to go in were bigger you put another sleeper in at the back and hammered a couple of irons in to keep it in place - that was your bigger standing. Granddad kept Shorthorns and Blue Albions. There was a lean-to which was divided up and tied 12 calves and a bull with little swinging doors in quite a small space. There was also a big mere on the yard. On the other side is what we call a Linney - a Devon term for a lean-to shed.

The Barn Below House was where uncle milked cows; he changed the traditional format to a lengthways shippon to get more cows in.

On the land called Maltby Tops are two barns - the top barn is my favourite. We kept four stirks in there; every day we'd go over and let them out two at a time to water and clean up, then let them back in and let two more out, then hay them all. We didn't go much for bedding; they had to make do with the wooden standings.

The bottom barn at Maltby Tops was bigger; it tied 8, so it was down to that and do the same; they got very well trained an you got up the little ladder and put the hay down through the holes in the baulks floor into the racks. Each barn had its own mer and its surround of hay meadows to make a little unit.

Whitewashing was a wet day job after turnout. I've never understood why it looks grey when you put it on and then you tur your back and it's dazzling white. From the 15th-20th April the swallows come but one thing I would miss at Paradise ar skylarks - if I couldn't hear one on a summer day it would break my heart.

Come haytime, anybody who was around was roped in; we had relatives who used to come for a 'fun' day on the farm an Douglas worked on the farm for many years from being a lad of 14. Granny must have thought a lot of him because she mad him 'Shartin' bread.

Uncle mowed with a reciprocating blade horse mower and then granddad and I mostly - we were very close - walked roun the field tedding it out where it was thicker. If it looked like rain we'd coil it up and I had a few good lessons about coiling becaus if I didn't get it right, granddad would get irritated and snap, 'Do it like this with a proper cap on it!' - it was about four forkfuls a little round heap with a lid on. Then when you were ready you could flick it over on its back to dry the bottom and often tha would do the trick and then you could carry it.

We used to put it loose onto the cart with the gormers on the end and it was quite a posh job being the hay loader, and whe you got better you could work on the front end - you always did that a bit heavier to take some strain off the horse.

As a girl it was my job unfortunately to be the one to go right into the roof where they used to poke the hay at you. It wa sticky and hay seeds all over you and you'd say, 'That's enough.' And they'd say 'Just another one.' You were thumping it dow with your knees which were itching like mad by then. Tea tasted wonderful after that!

*Above left,
Maltby Tops,
top barn*

*Above right,
Top Barn*

Barn Below House

Maltby Tops, top barn

Barn Below House

Lea Barn. Ollerbrook, Edale

I've lived here all my life at Ollerbrook and m
dad and grandfather before me. We used Le
Barn for young cattle; it tied 27 at one time the
we altered one half of it to take dry cows. W
went down twice a day to fodder them an
turned them out for water in the afternoor
When grandfather got past it, I went one end o
the day when I was a lad. Dad's pals woul
come and 'kall' when they knew you wer
waterin', fodderin' or muckin' out - for a gossi
because there were no telephones.

We did it all up then the hiker problem started
We'd always had the odd person sleep in, do n
damage and go but the bad element came an
that's when we made provision up here for th
young cattle. We let them run in and out of th
barn for a while and then we locked it up.

Lands Barn

It was run with Middle Ollerbrook. It was sold and Brown Bailey Steelworks bought it. They altered it and put a new loft floor in - ruined the barn really but now it is better for us. We work with sheep in it away from the footpaths; it's a lot easier for us. You have a job to do any work with stock in the yard now because of the sheer volume of visitors passing through. Many have no sense as to how to act and do not even acknowledge you.

J W and C M Thornley

Lea Barn, Grindsbrook

Lose Hill Barn

Every one round here knew Lose Hill Farm as Crimea. In the 1940s and 50s a man called Jim McCarthy lived there. He was well known as a bit of a character and he walked everywhere; he hadn't a vehicle and his daughters did the same. It was a hard life; they had no electricity. Just after the war they put in a little windmill to provide electricity but it didn't last long up there; soon blew away. The house was very basic.

He used to go to Bakewell Market and buy calves - roan shorthorns - and someone would bring them home for him. He reared them to 2 years old then he'd sell them to us to finish for the butchers shop. He'd only sell one at a time; we'd go up to see him of a night. We rarely got up to the house; he'd see you and come down and meet you with a lantern. We'd make him an offer and then he'd walk it down for you. He made hay in the 2 meadows round the barn and tied about 10 stirks in there in winter. There was always water in the ditch in winter but we struggle for water in the summer.

Robert Watson

New Barn, Whitmore Lea, Barber Booth, Edale.

In the meadow we used a hay sweep, a tumble pulled by the horse, either Bob or Dolly. John Neil

haw Wood Barn

haw Wood Barn and Meadow Head Barn are on land which used to belong to the Carrington family at Ivy house Farm, next to e chapel at Barber Booth. They were milking in shippons which are now private dwellings or holiday cottages. The house too has ow gone out of farming so there are just the two barns left as agricultural buildings of which we bought Meadow Head and the urrounding land some years ago.

I spent all my time on our farm; my husband was ill and I remember it was lonely work. I could be up the fields there thinking it ould be nice if Jim could come up for a chat.

There used to be another little cote up the bank side near the moor. We just called it The Cote and I believe years ago cattle ere kept up there and geese. My mother-in-law used to say it was excellent for sheep to shelter in off the moors. The farm has een in the family since the 1600s and that plot was walled in but now with the aid of tourists there is hardly anything left.

Haymaking at the barns was by hand; you'd ted it all out and then it would rain. I do remember putting it up in little 'coils'; you ent along the row and it was like a forkful this way and a fork that way and it just kept the wet out and then we coiled it up into igger 'cocks' at night to keep it dry.

Belinda Critchlow

Meadow Head Barn, Edale

Upper Booth Barns

We lived at Upper Booth Farm for 21 years from 1959. Colonel Haythornthwaite was the owner of the farm; he was from Lancashire and was a very good and kind landlord to us. When he died the farm was left to the National Trust.

The barn near Crowden Clough we knew as Newfield Barn. We used it for storing hay and there were 2 small shippons at each end which fed 6 small stirks. In the early days the hay was gathered loose; we loaded it onto a dray and took it to the barn. I can remember one year having to get the hay a bit green because the weather looked like breaking and there was steam coming up through the roof slates.

New Field Barn - Crowden Barn

Cowhay Barn used to go with Lee farm which had belonged to the NT for many years. The meadow there always grew good red clover. The barn was renovated in the 1960s and used by Nottingham Education Authority for outdoor pursuits for school groups.

Mallinsons were at Orchard Farm and milked cows at the barn there and Smiths were at Dalehead and sent milk from there too. Harold Johnson milked at The Lee; he never had more than a churn and that rarely full. He used to bring it down to our milk stand in an Armstrong Siddeley which was a massive saloon car. In fact just about every farm in Edale sent milk but we were the first to give up in 1964. People thought we were mad because we were giving up a regular income. *Eileen Hodgson.*

Gate Barn (same as Cowhay Barn - see EH) is near the old packhorse route from Edale over Edale Cross to Hayfield. (*Gate was sometimes used for an old track such as the nearby Chapel Gate SH*) I would think it was built in the early 1800s when the land round Upper Booth was enclosed and improved. This house (Upper Booth) was built in 1830 and used to be called Shaw Ground Farm at Crowden Booth.

In Crowden Barn (also known as Newfield Barn) are the old stone remains of a thrashing floor.

There is a field barn in the area known as The Intake close to Whitemoor Clough and once part of Dalehead Farm.

Robert Helliwell.

Crowden Barn

Cowhay - Gate Barn

Yarncliffe Barn, Longshaw

18th century origins with 19th century rebuild a further additions in the l 19th century. There a earthwork remains of medieval house(s) directly the south of the barn. T landscape in this area w radically changed in the ea 19th century when large pa of common moorland we enclosed - this includes area around the barn.

National Tr

oadhole Cote, Crookhill Farm, Hope Woodlands

he site includes a couple of field barns. Earliest reference for Crookhill is from between 1101 and 1108 - although this may just efer to a topographical feature from which the farm takes its name. In the 13th century a monastic grange was assarted from the oyal Forest at Crookhill by Welbeck Abbey. It is believed, although not definitive, that Crookhill is the most likely location of this range. The property was let to Thomas Eyre in the early 15th century and remained in the Eyre family until the early 19th century, espite the dissolution of the monasteries when Welbeck's lands were passed to the Earl of Shrewsbury. Crookhill then formed art of the Devonshire or Chatsworth Estate, until the early 20th century when it was acquired by the Derwent Valley Water Board. oadhole Cote, 400m south-east of the farmstead appears to have replaced an earlier building, and is now used as an informal vestock shelter. The interior has a small loose box or shippon and a larger shippon originally for fifteen standings. *National Trust*

Toadhole Cote

Barn at Common Plants Wood, Hassop

Wheatlands Barn, Wheatlands Lane near Baslow

Barn on Birchill Farm near Pilsley

By Bradley Lane, Pilsley. Left, 1999, and right, October 2011

The Parthenon, Chatsworth

arn by Long Rake Spar

'e often see a bus full of Oriental people stop at the side of the road and they all get out and take photographs of our barn. It has
en mentioned in the National Geographic photographic section.

Trevor Broadhurst, Long Rake Spar Co.

Bonsall Barns

On the south-east edge of the Peak District is the village of Bonsall situated within an area which was extensively lead mined. Concentrated in this area are many field barns; a survey in 1985 found that there were still 117 in an area of 2 x 3 miles. These were built from the time of enclosure up to the late 1800s; each barn unique in size and design.

Quite often a barn is sited near to a mine shaft, the farmer/miner working seasonally. These small stone sheds are called a 'coe' where miners could shelter, keep food, working clothes, tools and 'bing ore' - large pieces of high grade ore. This was often stored and from here could be measured and sold. Early coes were thatched.

Many of these barns as elsewhere were falling into decay and being lost and a resident of the village, Liz Stoppard was concerne that an important part of our heritage was slipping away. To cut a long story short Liz was motivated to do something and so alor with George Caldicot and Mike Susko she got the community behind a project to restore some of the barns and the Bonsall Barr Project was born. In the first year, 2005 a pilot project was carried out where 3 barns were restored for £15,000. Grant fundir was obtained from the Aggregates Levy with help from volunteers and local farmers as match funding. In all, £65,000 was use to restore over 20 barns including a miner's coe and lengths of drystone walling and gates.

In some cases Welsh slate has been obtained and used because it was reasonably priced and is difficult to steal compared stone slates or Staffordshire Blue tiles. It also looks better than tin sheets. Several barns that had no roof or timbers and gable partly broken down have been restored including loft and steps for about £2,500 each.

The team would like to continue restoring barns but have so far been unable to access further funding because of red tape.

Some Bonsall barns

Off Salters Lane, left, 2004, and right, 2011 - restored using £14000 funding

Off Salters Lane, Bonsall

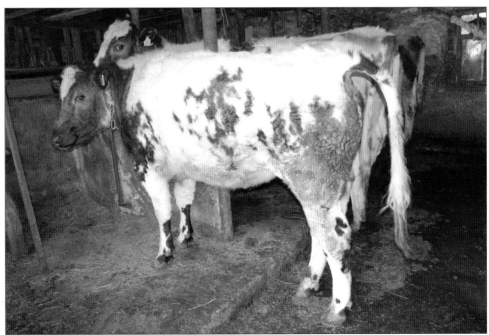

143

AND FINALLY....

Now you are at the end of this book you will have an appreciation of how and why the field barns of the Peak District came abou and were developed. There is only room for a sample of the many barns which survive but even so we can see the wonderfu variety of them and the range of individual rugged beauty, reflecting their history and varied function. It is this great variety farming circumstances which has led to the current situation where some farmers have been able to keep the buildings in repa and use, perhaps with modification, and some have failed. The modern pressure to intensify, the necessary use of large moder livestock buildings and increasingly bigger machinery, and the loss of men on the ground has led to so many of the outer building falling out of use, or worse into a state of dereliction.

When I started this project I thought that in the present economic circumstances it might be difficult to justify the expense of proper repairs and restoration of field barns, many of which now have little agricultural value. However as I have gone around I have noticed that many are valuable habitats for wildlife and birds - owls and swallows especially. With the conversion of traditional farmstead buildings to domestic or other non-farming uses and the construction of modern buildings that swallows rarely seem to use, it seems these outlying buildings have become even more valuable.

The barns are also widely appreciated by the non-farming community for their landscape value; you have only got to look on internet sites like 'Flickr' to see the many photographs that people take of field barns in the landscape. So it seems sensible that grant-aid should be made available to preserve a valuable asset that is in a lot of cases slipping away.

Since the 1980s there have been 3 main national agri-environment schemes - first Environmentally Sensitive Areas (ESAs then Countryside Stewardship (CSS) and now Environmental Stewardship (ESS). In the early days, in ESAs, quite a lot of barr were repaired - the requirements and conditions were relatively few and were easily met, the costs were not particularly hig and the 80% grant made it easier to afford. Often the work was done by local building firms and the funds stayed in the localit contributing to the local economy. As time and the schemes have progressed, the approaches have developed an Environmental Stewardship Schemes, delivered through Natural England on behalf of Defra, are now much more focused o the use of traditional materials and time-honoured skills; the aim being to keep the buildings functional and as close to th original as possible.

One result of these developments, along with increasing concerns about liabilities, is that the process has become mor complex, competitive (because of limited available funding), lengthy and inevitably more expensive, particularly in the early stage when there is no guarantee that the project will go ahead but investment has nevertheless to be made in order to produce th

Barn on Arkwright Square land, near Pike Hall

aperwork to make the case for the proposal. Some projects don't get funding and some farmers have withdrawn because of the increasing costs. Another side effect of the increase in costs is that local builders aren't always able to tackle such expensive projects because of the paperwork and cash-flow issues.

So while we appreciate the restoration of these wonderful vernacular buildings to their former glory using traditional materials and skills, in the wider field there are still many barns being lost which could potentially be saved through a 'cheap and cheerful' process like the Bonsall Barns Project. After all some of these barns have been re-developed and adapted over a couple of centuries by farmers. Some of these projects could also be used as a training ground for young people to learn traditional and sustainable skills, like the use of lime mortar; whilst the extra work for our local builders would result in more income for the rural economy.

In 1988 the 'SAVE' report expressed concern about the demolition of farm buildings and crude conversions which destroy the special architectural and historic interest. It illustrated some of the uses to which farm buildings could be put and urged that conversion must respect the character and fabric of the original building. Lessons could be learned from the late 1950s and 1960s when money was pumped into grant aiding new buildings as farmers were encouraged to increase production, and old buildings were neglected and as they attracted no aid, a lot were swept away to make room for the new ones.

Cruck Barn holiday cottage, Hartington

Even in 1988 the report acknowledged that farmers faced such uncertainty with the EU calling the shots that even in a few months situations could change. This seems even more poignant now.

Architect Tony Busfield when asked his opinion about the conversion of field barns offered, 'Once you have a domestic building you are surrounded by all the trappings of domesticity such as cars, washing and children's toys so it no longer looks like or serves the purpose of a rural agricultural building. For alternative rural use like a rural craft activity I would accept a track to the barn as a compromise. In some cases near roadsides, or in the curtilage of a village, conversion may be applicable, but then some people can throw a lot of money at a conversion and everything special is lost - they become twee and not rural.'

SAVE recognised that where planning permission is given for residential development and conditions attached to prevent 'suburban paraphernalia' these conditions are hardly ever enforced and a compatible use in the location may well conflict with others such as traffic, access and services.

Within the Peak District National Park, the relevant planning policies note that barn conversions will only be looked at favourably where the buildings lie within settlements, that outlying barns won't be considered because of the dangers of 'domesticating' the rural landscape with just the sort of paraphernalia referred to above, destroying the character of the landscapes that so many people, whether visitors or residents, enjoy so much.

Butterlands camping barn

There are some well converted holiday cottages and some people who have successfully converted barns to camping barns or bunk barns. They are also known as 'stone tents'. Essentially the outsides stay simple and unspoiled. Living and sleeping areas are usually communal though the barns can be booked for sole use. Accommodation is very simple with a sleeping platform, tables and benches, a supply of cold running water and a flush toilet. Many have basic heating such as a wood stove and some have hot water, shower and cooking facilities.

Some barns still have some agricultural use, whether for shelter for stock, somewhere to catch and handle stock or for storage, especially where they have been restored. We have established that they are a valuable part of our landscape heritage and our social history, they are important habitats for wildlife and are heritage assets in their own right, so it is a shame that despite the best efforts of so many people and organisations that more buildings can't be saved. What we need is more of the people who have come to admire these buildings to express their concerns to their elected representatives their MPs, County and District Councillors and National Park Authority Members, to seek to influence them to find more, better and cheaper ways of restoring these buildings that are, on the one hand so relatively common, but on the other so important for helping current and future generations to appreciate how the landscape has come to look like it does, how it was and is still being worked and why these buildings are an important part of the Peak District's and this country's heritage.

The old and the new. New Buildings in New Buildings field, Oddo House Farm, Elton

Barn at Onecote

ACKNOWLEDGEMENTS

My thanks to all the people, too many to name individually, who have allowed me access to their land and supplied information and encouragement.

My thanks also to the Peak District National Park Authority for grant aid towards my expenses, to Ken Smith, Brian Rich and Rachael Hall (National Trust), and to Annie and Tony at Delmar Press